WE ARE BRIGHTON
PLAY OFF SPECIAL

© Bennett Dean

Bennett Dean has asserted his rights in accordance with the Copyright, Designs and Patents Act 1988 to be identified as the author of this work.

Publishing By:
Pitch Publishing (Brighton) Ltd
10 Beresford Court
Somerhill Road
Hove BN3 1RH
Email: info@pitchpublishing.co.uk
Web: www.pitchpublishing.co.uk

First published 2004.

A catalogue record for this book is available from the British Library.

ISBN 0-9542460-7-1

All pictures by Bennett Dean, except for the following:
John Elms: pages 10 (both), 11, 27, 81 (top right)

Printed and bound in Great Britain by East Sussex Press

Acknowledgements

In no particular order I would like to thank John Hopkins, John Elms, Andrew Hawes, Graham Rolfe, Sky Sports, the Three Jolly Butchers, Pitch, and everyone – the players, management, staff and supporters – at the Albion for their help and assistance.

Biggest thanks of all, however, go to the BDs at Seagulls World: Paul, Tim, Nicky and Ferret, who helped make the season one of the most memorable of my life.

See you in Division One.

Bennett Dean

WE ARE BRIGHTON

PLAY OFF SPECIAL

Bennett Dean

Foreword by Dick Knight

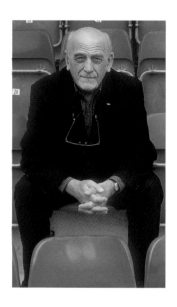

As an aspiring advertising copywriter, one of the skills I honed was the ability to write scripts for television ads. As my career progressed, those ads were evolving: moving away from old-fashioned 'pack-shot'campaigns to the more artistic and involving commercials we see today - more like mini films; films which required the most creative of scripts to make real impact in such a short space of time.

Throughout the 1970s and 1980s, many of my peers in the business took their scriptwriting and producing skills across the Atlantic to Hollywood – and once there set about creating gripping blockbuster movies. However, even these creative geniuses could not have penned a script that dripped with the drama we've seen unfold at the Albion in the past few years.

Any producer will tell you a good script only becomes a great one with a fine cast. Here at Brighton we've enjoyed a cast of absolute stars. Some have been only cameo roles, some more sustained, while others have felt unable to fulfil their personal ambitions at a football club hamstrung by its nomadic existence. They have moved on to bigger and better things, but not before they've been involved in some memorably thrilling seasons; and it's a measure of what we've achieved that they still hold the Albion close to their hearts.

It's fair to say, we've also had our share of heartache; but nail-biting delays over the new stadium and relegation from Division One last time we were at this level will only make us even more determined to succeed as we head into 2004/05.

Last season was another thriller, but the first with such an intriguing and exciting finale. Shortly after arriving on the south coast Mark McGhee predicted that the season would go right to the wire... he couldn't have been more spot on. On that day the cast was in excess of 30,000 and the football world saw the potential of this football club as we capped a fine season with the unforgettable experience of the Millennium Stadium.

Enjoy this look back - through the lens of club photographer Bennett Dean - but remember if we're to see a real Albion blockbuster, first we must have the theatre and surroundings in which the people of Brighton, Hove and Sussex can view it properly.

We Want Falmer!

Dick Knight

"Going to the Albion is something I do.
I'll only stop when I die."

Albion fan Graham Rolfe

"This will be a mental and physical grind over the next nine months. I think we're up for it, but that will only show come three o'clock Saturday and in the fixtures after that."

Albion manager Steve Coppell

"If you get into the right positions, and the balls are right, then you're going to score goals."

Albion striker Leon Knight

"He shot, he scored, he's only five foot four... Leon Knight..."

Albion fans at Oldham rework an old terrace anthem for their new hero

"I've always conformed to the Ron Atkinson school of management when it comes to penalties: whoever is confident grabs the ball and takes it. The problem was there were two confident players, but given the difference in stature of the players it was no accident Darius took it!"

Albion manager Steve Coppell

"I was very impressed by Plymouth when they beat us 2-0 at Home Park, but the best was Brighton's second-half performance at the Withdean early in the season. They passed us off the park and beat us 2-1."

QPR manager Ian Holloway on the best performance against his team

"I was so pleased for him...
I said to him ten minutes before the
game that he's got nothing to prove to
any of these people... he's come in today and
done a magnificent job. There's no-one more
than me who wants to pat him on the back."

**Albion midfielder Charlie Oatway on Guy
Butters's return from the wilderness**

Neither side deserved to lose a terrific game of football. Most Albion fans would probably have settled for a point before the start, and the point is likely to look like one gained, rather than two lost, as the season moves on."

Seagull matchday magazine

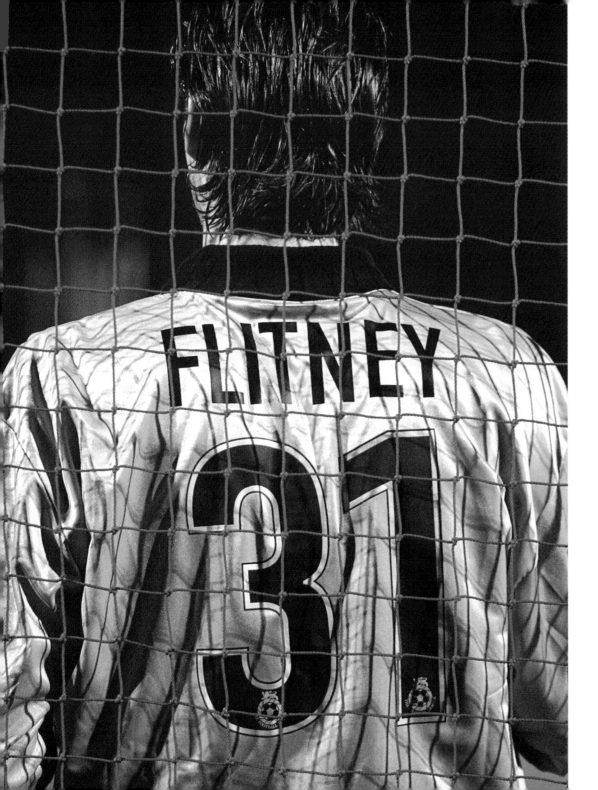

"A back injury to Ben Roberts has forced Steve Coppell to hand loan keeper Ross Flitney his first senior start for the visit of Chesterfield."
Albion's official website

"Ross came in and except for one little aberration I think it was a terrific performance."
Albion manager Steve Coppell

"It will be good. I only found out this morning that I was coming back, but I am very pleased. I went to Hull to get some games under my belt. It has definitely benefited me, as first-team games are always better than reserve-team games and I feel I played well."
Albion goalkeeper Michel Kuipers on his recall from Hull City

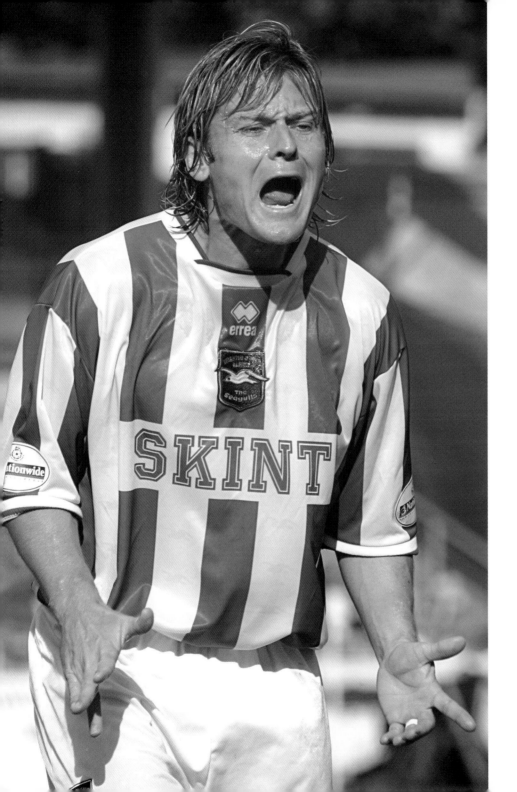

"I've done what I came to do."

Albion striker Leon Knight on scoring against former club Sheffield Wednesday

"Knight's on the edge of the area, goes for a shot with his left foot and drives in a fantastic goal... The shirt's off again for Leon Knight and Brighton are back in front."
Andrew Hawes *BBC Southern Counties' Radio*

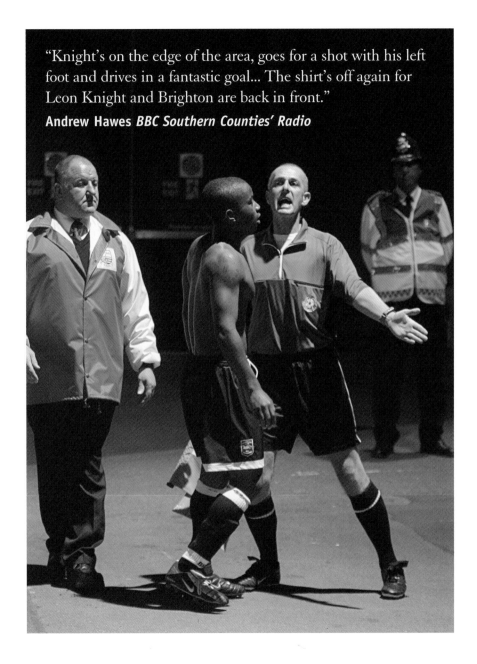

"I am torn. I've got something great going here.
If we had the stadium it wouldn't be an issue."

Albion manager Steve Coppell

"He's been involved in the squad for a few weeks now, and at his age – he was 17 on Thursday – there is a lot of psychological and mental strain when you join up with the first team. We need to look after all our young talent."

Albion caretaker manager Bob Booker

"Brighton & Hove Albion are pleased to announce Mark McGhee as the new manager of the club. He has signed a two-year contract and takes charge with immediate effect..."

Albion press release

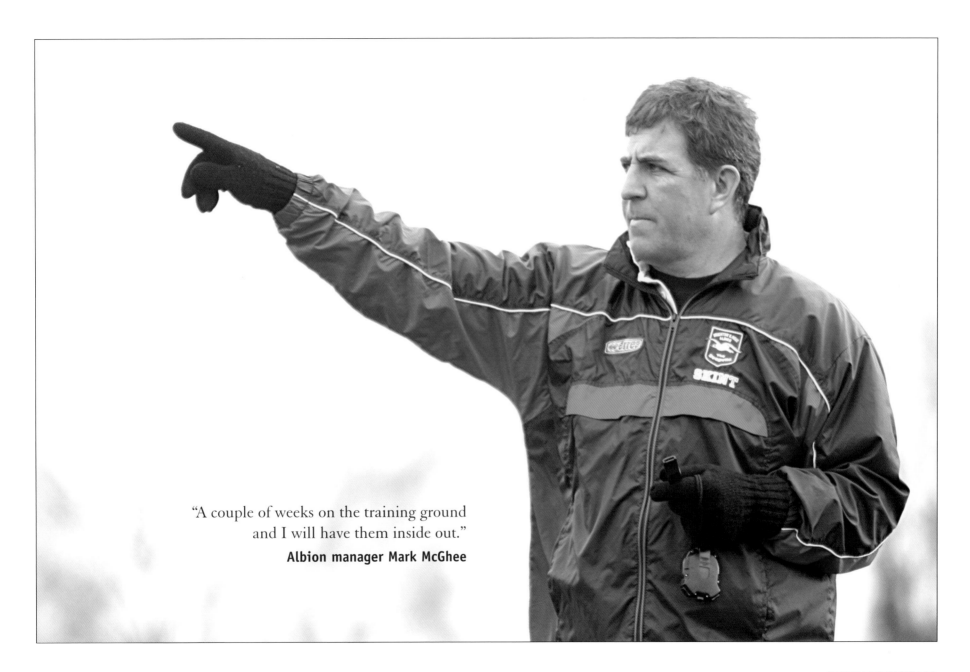

"A couple of weeks on the training ground
and I will have them inside out."
Albion manager Mark McGhee

"He let us know what he wants and in return he'll give a lot back to us. We can't wait until Saturday; I know the boys are going to be gee'd up for it. With a new manager coming in, individuals want to show what they can do, and as a team we want to show what we can do. So I think we'll be on our game on Saturday."

Albion striker Leon Knight

"I enjoyed the afternoon immensely. I got a nice reception from the supporters, which pleased me. I'm very glad to be here and I'm looking forward to the rest of the season."

Albion manager Mark McGhee

"I think that there is certainly some tweaking that needs to be done."

Albion manager Mark McGhee

"Brighton are my team and a part of my life. The idea that it might not be if we don't have anywhere permanent to play is quite worrying, which is why I am here today."

Albion fan Norman Cook

"I think it is important to show the depth of feeling in Brighton & Hove about this new ground."

Albion fan Des Lynam

"Listen to the people Mr Prescott! No other application in the history of Brighton & Hove has had so much evidenced support – the people are behind the new stadium!"

Albion fan Paul Samrah

"It's been over 14 months since my last start, so when the gaffer came up to me and said that I was going to start at right-back I was delighted, because I have put in a lot of hard work to get back into the team since Steve Coppell left, and I think I got my just reward."

Albion defender Adam Virgo

44 BARNSLEY AT HOME

"I think it was handball. I think the referee has seen it, although he hasn't given it. I was very disappointed with the referee in that respect. It was a big decision and I felt that he didn't have the courage to make it. Big decisions change games and that was a turning point in the sense that had we had a 1-0 lead then, against ten men, it would have made all the difference."

Mark McGhee on the referee's decision not to award Albion a penalty at QPR

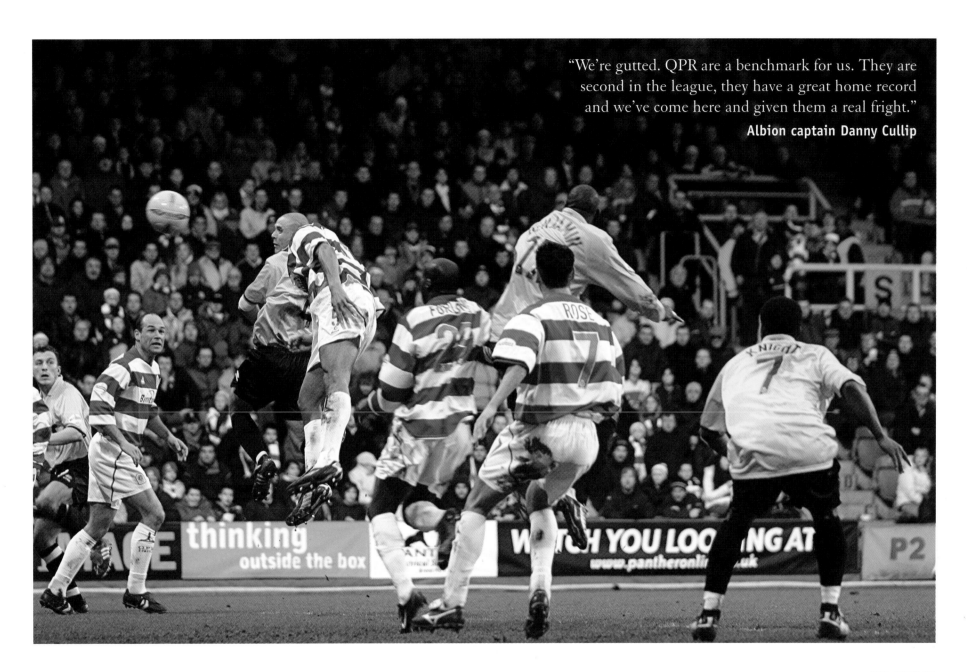

"We're gutted. QPR are a benchmark for us. They are second in the league, they have a great home record and we've come here and given them a real fright."

Albion captain Danny Cullip

SAVE BRIGHTON

LISTEN TO THE PEOPLE
MR PRESCOTT

www.ClubsInCrisis.com

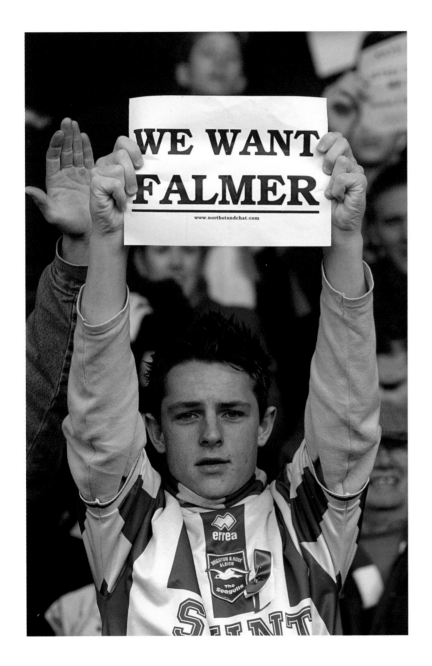

"Once again Albion fans have risen to the occasion. It was an absolutely brilliant response to our call. Today is another landmark in the history of the Albion in terms of the fantastic support that we have, and I hope that John Prescott gets the message and gives us the right decision."

Albion chairman Dick Knight

"A club like Brighton & Hove Albion, with the tradition that it has, deserves a proper venue in which to run out in the Football League. We've come to Wycombe today, and they've got a ground to be proud of; and yet their tradition is nothing like the tradition of Brighton & Hove Albion."

Albion manager Mark McGhee

"You have to be preparing for a game like this way ahead of it. You can't turn up here tonight and think that you can just turn on the gas – you have to prepare after the game on Saturday.

"You have got to be at home on Saturday night, putting your feet up and resting. The same goes for Sunday, preparing and training on Sunday, as we did. And then more training on Monday and thinking about it and really getting yourself determined for the game.

"That's what we should be doing, but I think that we are turning up at some of these games and we are really only starting to get up for it an hour and a half before the game, and that has really not been good enough."

Albion manager Mark McGhee

61, 452
people voted
STADIUM YES
listen to
the people
Mr Prescott

"Jonesy just hit a great ball to the back post and I just jumped and it hit my head. I didn't know what to do with the celebration. I was a bit shocked to have scored."
Albion defender Adam Virgo

"If you had said at the start of the season that we would be in the play-off places at this stage then we would have settled for that. There are still 12 games to go and if we can remain there then it will have been a good season for us."

Albion midfielder Richard Carpenter

"Iwelumo with a curling shot... a sensational debut goal from Chris Iwelumo from 25 yards. Whipped it past Muggleton right into the corner and Brighton are surely heading for their first away win since November."

Andrew Hawes
BBC Southern Counties' Radio

"I've had a few (long-range goals) and hopefully there will be more, but I'll take any goal. If it's off my bum or whatever I'm not bothered."

Albion striker Chris Iwelumo

"I'm delighted to have joined a team with ambition, both for the play-offs and also further ahead. Hopefully everything will go through with the Falmer stadium. It's been a step forward for me.

"I'm settling in well. The lads have been brilliant, absolutely outstanding, and have made me feel like I've been part of the dressing room for a long time."

Albion striker Chris Iwelumo

"We have had games this season when we have ended up drawing games like this, and all I can say is that on a day when we did not play too well, I think the difference between drawing and winning was that we had a player in Chris Iwelumo who is going to make a little bit of difference to us."

Albion manager Mark McGhee

"Chris and I complement each other. The week before last he set me up against Colchester, and he just tells me to get around him and pick up the little bits and pieces that he will try and flick on.

"He wins a lot in the air and he talks a lot, and you can hear him talking to all the players. He's a motivator and he's not afraid to say what he sees. I like to play with those sort of players."

Albion striker Leon Knight

"This 0-0 draw with Bristol City is indicative of how far Albion have come since Mark McGhee took over as manager. When the Robins romped to a 4-1 win at Withdean back in November there was an enormous gulf between the two sides, but not so today, and after 90 hard minutes you could hardly separate these play-off contenders."

Albion's official website

"It feels a bit weird to be honest! The best I've ever done was runner-up at Gillingham, but to actually win it is a new experience for me and a nice feeling!"

Albion player-of-the-season Guy Butters

"The award completes an amazing turnaround for Butters: this time last year he was the forgotten man: out on loan at Barnet, out of favour and had slipped down the defensive pecking order."

Albion's official website

"I think he's a credit to himself, and an example to older players of the rewards hard work can bring."

Albion manager Mark McGhee

"Sometimes this year away from home we've been unfortunate, where we've played really well and haven't got the results. Maybe our luck is changing a little bit. It's about time we had some luck away from home."

Albion defender Guy Butters

"We went to their place and got what we expected, but we stuck to our game plan and limited them to just a couple of chances, so I was very comfortable with the way we played the game.

"I would have settled for a 1-0 deficit going back to our place, but we've done well enough to get a victory. Now we take Swindon back to our place with a 1-0 advantage, but we have to make sure we don't lose our concentration."

Albion manager Mark McGhee

"Winning this match tonight would give us our greatest opportunity yet to demonstrate why the City of Brighton and Hove needs and deserves a stadium. Where better than in a final at the Millennium Stadium to make our voices heard?

"However, before that becomes a reality we have the task of overcoming a wounded but still determined Swindon side. They have argued we were lucky and actually did not defend well (given their 3 chances).

"I was happy. Our defending was organised, determined and resilient. We stayed the distance even though we took a couple of punches. To claim that the woodwork saved us is clutching at straws a bit... Tonight we will give it our best and I am sure Swindon will do similar... MAY THE LUCKIEST TEAM WIN!"

Mark McGhee's play-off semi-final programme notes

"The 30 minutes are almost up Swindon fans, but you're not there yet... in it goes... ohhhhhh it's gone in! Brighton in added-on time have snatched a goal through Virgo!"

Ian Crocker *Sky Sports*

"I'm absolutely thrilled with that. Believe you me, anyone who has bought one of those tickets will not regret it.

"They will remember the experience – particularly if we win – but they will remember the experience. It's a fantastic place and well worthy of hosting these games."

Mark McGhee reacting to news that the Albion had sold over 25,000 tickets in the first two days of sales

2 PLAY-OFFS
20 04
MILLENNIUM STADIUM, CARDIFF
errea
BRIGHTON & HOVE ALBION
The Seagulls
errea
BRIGHTON & HOVE ALBION
The Seagulls

"I was so excited to get out, I was like a kid on Christmas Eve, you know. I just wanted to get out and play. If I want to play at the top I've got to play under the biggest pressure."

Albion defender Adam Virgo

"It's a magnificent day and for anyone who hasn't been there, when they walk into that stadium it will just take their breath away.

"When the teams come out and the noise erupts then, for the people of Brighton, who have not had that experience at a decent stadium, it will really be something new for them."

Albion manager Mark McGhee

"Here he comes... and Leon Knight fires Brighton in front... and fires the dream, the dream of promotion to Division One."

Ian Crocker *Sky Sports*

"Massive moment for that young man. All the hopes are resting on his shoulders. The noise in the stadium didn't put him off... That takes a lot of guts, a lot of bravery. You're looking for a hero and it looks like he could be the one."

Garry Birtles *Sky Sports*

"They've got what they hoped for.
They've got what they prayed for.
They've got what they came for.
Brighton are promoted to the
First Division. Up, up and away!"

Ian Crocker *Sky Sports*

"It was just amazing. Coming here on the coach through the streets with all the fans outside the pubs – the back of my neck was up."

Albion assistant manager Bob Booker

"You can't bottle what this club has got."

Albion midfielder Charlie Oatway

"The crowd just went crazy, our whole team went crazy."

Albion striker Leon Knight

"It was a fantastic day out, and once again the supporters were an absolute credit to the club, the players and the city of Brighton & Hove.

"The Albion supporters created a wonderful atmosphere in Cardiff, cheered the team throughout the match and showed John Prescott exactly why they deserve a proper stadium in which to watch their team.

"The array of Falmer banners looked fantastic. It was a brilliant effort and the potential this club has – something we have been telling John Prescott all about – was there for all to see."

Albion chairman Dick Knight

"It's a fantastic achievement given everything that has gone on, and is going on. The boys have worked really hard for it.

"It's not always been pretty, it's not always been convincing, it's not always been certain – but they've kept at it and their attitude has been magnificent. We've won the important one!"

Albion manager Mark McGhee

"We had a thing up in the changing room: a list of (First Division) stadiums one side and the Second Division the other side. We all want to be playing at the Walkers Stadium, Elland Road and thank God we are. Hopefully now we can get a ground like that."

Albion striker Leon Knight